Ruth's Promise

A Tale of Loyalty, Love, and God's Faithfulness

Extraordinary women of the bible journal series

Natouchka L. Voigt

Ruth's Promise

Copyright © 2025 Natouchka L. Voigt

All rights reserved.

ISBN:979-8-9929167 0-6

About The Book

RUTH'S PROMISE serves as a heartfelt message to those who are trusting God while navigating questions and uncertainties.

It speaks to those seeking His path, growing in their faith, and believing in His promises. This journey reminds us that in the end, we will see God's promises fulfilled and witness our legacy unfold.

Ruth's Promise

About The Author

Natouchka Voigt is a mother of five, a Pastor in New York, a public speaker, and a business coach. With a passion for helping people from all walks of life discover the love of Christ, she has committed herself to community service and spiritual mentorship.

Pastor Voigt empowers individuals to overcome challenges, build their faith, and lead purposeful lives.

Her message resonates with authenticity and compassion, reflecting her deep commitment to making a difference in the lives of others.

Dedication

I dedicate this lovely book to my first grandchild, Genesis-Joy. I also dedicate it to my daughters, Jasmine and Nagee, and all the daughters who have and shall cross my path. May they continue to grow in faith, embrace God's promises, and see his glorious purpose for their lives.

Prologue

In the days when the Judges ruled Israel, there was a famine in the land, and the house of Elimelech from Bethlehem was forced to leave their homeland and seek refuge in Moab. Little did Naomi, Elimelech's wife, know that this journey would lead her through the darkest chapters of grief and loss. First, her husband died in Moab: Naomi's two sons, Mahlon and Chilion, married women from the land—Ruth and Orpah. But tragedy struck again, and Naomi lost her sons, leaving her with only her daughters-in-law.

Naomi was devastated and alone and decided to return to Bethlehem, hearing that the Lord had visited His people with food.
In this moment of despair, Ruth, Naomi's Moabite first daughter-in-law, made a vow of loyalty that would forever alter her fate. Ruth's heart was bound to Naomi, and despite the grief, she chose to stay with her, leaving behind the familiar world of Moab and her own family. Naomi, disheartened by her losses and uncertain of what the future held, tried to send Ruth away, but Ruth refused.

The journey back to Bethlehem was not an easy one. Ruth, a foreign widow, would be walking into a land where customs, laws, and traditions were foreign to her. Yet, her love and commitment to Naomi carried her through each step.

Bethlehem, a place of both sorrow and hope, awaited their return. The path ahead was fraught with uncertainty, but Ruth's faith and Naomi's wisdom would guide them.

Ruth's story is not merely a tale of loss but transformation. It is the story of a young woman who, through devotion and faith, chose to embrace the God of Israel and the people of Naomi, even when the odds were against her. With each entry of this journal, Ruth's journey unfolds—marked by preparation, customs, dreams, tribulations, and a new beginning. From her humble laboring in the fields to her encounter with Boaz, the kinsman redeemer, Ruth's faithfulness would lead her into a future filled with unexpected grace and divine purpose.

This is the story of Ruth—a tale of a woman bound by love and faith, and a journey that would ultimately restore hope to a broken family and change the course of history.

Ruth's journal is not just a record of her journey but a testimony to the redeeming power of God and the faith that can bloom even in the most unlikely of places.
As you read, walk alongside Ruth in her moments of grief and joy, their doubts and triumphs, as their faithfulness guides her through the unknown and into the promise of restoration. Her journey is one of courage, resilience, and the deep love that can only come from trusting God's providence.
Ruth Journal and Journey tell the tale of loss, restoration, and the grace that can emerge from even the darkest times.

The Outline

About The Book

About the author

Dedication

Prologue

Outline
Entry 1:   The Preparation
Entry 2:   The Dream and Customs
Entry 3:   Naomi's Way & Faith
Entry 4:   Do It with Grace
Entry 5:   Though I have a mother
Entry 6:   It's been 10 Years
Entry 7:   Being an Outcast
Entry 8:   My Husband Mahlon
Entry 9:   Test & Tribulation
Entry 10:   The Uncertainty
Entry 11:   The Dreadful Cloud
Entry 12:   The Visitor
Entry 13:   Returning To Bethlehem
Entry 14:   Our Journey
Entry 15:   Laboring In A Field
Entry 16:   The Kinsman Redeemer
Entry 17:   A Permanent Home
Entry 18:   The Meeting
Entry 19:   Joy Restored

Write your own Journal and leave a Legacy
The Scriptural verse
A Heartfelt Thank You

They were inseparable.

But I'm going to take you on a journey with Ruth long before there was a Boaz and long before there was a collapse of everything she came to know.

So, while you journey with me today, I hope you come to know Ruth as a friend. As we take this journey and read this journal that I put together based on her life, I hope you will be able to put yourself in Ruth's shoes to see her journey, healing, and triumph.

Welcome to Ruth's journey and journal.

Entry 1: The Preparation

I am Ruth, a Moabite, a widow, childless, and a woman who triumphs. This is my story.

When you think about Ruth in the Bible, people tend to think about Boaz,

Entry 2: The Dream and Customs

I, Ruth, as a young girl, always dreamt of what my wedding day would look like, the ceremony, the look on my mother's and father's faces. And the idea of marrying and caring for my children. I dream of that as I grow older, and to meet the person of my dreams. I never knew I would meet someone from the other side who would worship a different God than I.

As you know, the Moabites worship gods and idols. My husband is from Bethlehem. He believed in Judaism. And he believes in the true and living God. And they believe that one day, the Messiah will come. And all things were foreign to me. I never thought I would marry someone from the other side.

For sure, I thought he might be a Moabite like myself, of the same culture, of the same way of life. Never would have imagined he would be different, but life has a way of doing things very differently, and God has a way of introducing himself to us in various ways.

So, I started my journey and began my life, not knowing what would be ahead, but as I write this now, I remember the journey was never easy. Some of the dreams that I had would change, and some of the desires I had would change. There would be sorrowful moments. And then there would be joy. But as I record my memoirs, in my journal, as I record my life as a young woman, I remember that one day, I would come to know a God who is so merciful and gracious. He would become a father to me, a protector, and a provider. And he would change my life for the better.

Ruth's Promise

I reflect on the journey, I will meet my new family and my adult life will begin. I am in awe of what is in front of me, but what is in front of me is much deeper than what is on the surface. I can't wait to share my third entry with you as I progress to my wedding day.

Entry 3: Naomi's Way & Faith

I'm so excited that the preparation of my wedding is about to take place, trying to bring together two traditions and customs, my husband's, as well as my own, of the Moabites. After all, his family moved to Moab, and surely, they would adapt to our culture.

It was Elimelech and Naomi's desire for their 2 sons to marry, but they never imagined that their sons would marry Moabite women. This was not their preferred choice, but the famine that had taken place in Bethlehem had pushed them into Moab.
Moab is known for being a perpetual enemy of Israel.

What a stereotype on Moab, what a thing to carry, but it was true we were idol worshippers. It was full of adversity and sorrow. It was behavior that went against the Israelites' beliefs. The Israelites worshipped one God, Yahweh.

Yahweh is the name of their God, I would come to learn. I would also learn how to be a wife to my husband. Not only by the customs that I was taught by my mother and my mother's mother, but also as I watched and learned from my mother-in-law, Naomi's way

Naomi is such an amazing mother, no longer a mother-in-law but A MOTHER.

I have watched her pray to her God.
I have watched the calmness of her spirit.
I have watched her faith depend on God for all things. Provision, decision, and looking after her family.

Ruth's Promise

There was such a grace with Naomi, a grace we could only embrace. I am excited to share this because not only did I get married, but my sister also got married as well to my husband's brother.

Orpah also lived the dreams that we both dreamt as girls, to fall in love, to marry, and have children.

Every young girl dreams of marrying.
Every young girl dreams of bearing children of their own.
That was our most important role. I must repeat that in this entry because it is so important. I can't wait until I feel my child in my womb. I wait until I hold my child in my arms.

Entry 4: Do It with Grace

Though I had never met my father-in-law, Elimelech because he passed away before I became a part of the family. I can tell from the way my husband, Mahlon, and his brother Chilion are, it is clear that their ways as men resemble my father-in-law.

I can see from my mother-in-law, Naomi, that she truly loved him and was honored by his family.

Sometimes, Naomi goes off to a quiet place, and you can tell her heart is grieved from her loss. As I watched her continue to serve God, worship him, and kneel before him, she was never exhausted from being in his presence. I watched her in a quiet corner, observing her, and I learned.
The question that crosses my mind is, what and how does she keep pushing forward?

It is so unfortunate that when she came to Moab, my father-in-law died soon after, and she was left with her two sons in a foreign land and culture.

What a journey, what a process.

I am grateful to have been blessed with my husband. I watched him labor and lead the family, for me and his mother as well, because he is the oldest. I watched him do it with a strong back, powerful hands, and strength that surpassed what I could ask for.

So, as I continue to walk through my journey, watch and write everything down in my journal, I close my eyes at this moment and think of how blessed I am.

It isn't easy sometimes because we are also shunned from marrying outsiders.
It isn't easy for my husband or brother-in-law because they are looked upon differently and not received with open arms.

The Marketplace experience

My mother-in-law's experience when we go to a marketplace could be trying. People would look at her with evil eyes because she is not a Moabite. Sometimes the stares were because some of the women who had sons would have preferred Orpah and me to have been brides to their sons rather than going outside the culture. Other times, it would be jealousy because of the grace that was on her. Nonetheless, people would be people. But we must continue to live.
Naomi never shows that it bothers her. I know she misses her home, her culture, her tradition, the company of her family, and her friends. Naomi never wanted to leave her home or her family, and her friends.

I can imagine her back home at the well with her friends, laughing and enjoying each other's company.

I think it has been a bitter and painful moment for her to lose her husband who was what was left of home. She is no longer in her youth to remarry, so she depends on her sons and her inherited daughters. And we are grateful to do it for her because she has taught us all how to do it with grace.

Entry 5: Though I have a mother

Though I have my mother, as I watched Naomi, I saw the distinct differences between my mother and Naomi. I love my mother, but there is something about Naomi that has caused me to love her as if she were my birth mother.

I continue to grow as a woman through her.
I grew through our conversations and my quiet observation of her.

She treats us like we are daughters of her womb and with so much love. She is warm and welcoming.
As she teaches us about her God, she tells us that her God is redemptive. She tells us of her God having grace, love, and provisions. She explains that God shows up in all circumstances. As we sit in her presence, she helps us understand. I could stay there all day and drink up the wisdom of God that she gives, but of course, we have chores and responsibilities. Nonetheless, she always makes time for us to be fed and for us to come to understand the God her sons serve. And come to know the culture they came from, so that we may be able to love them and be present in the culture and traditions they grew up in.

As I sit and embrace those moments, when I watch my mother-in-law speak, there is a glow on her face. Her faith is like a bright light. It is contagious. How does she do it?
How does she get up daily without her husband and continue to press forward?

I could not imagine being without my husband. What would I do?
Well, I won't think of those things. I will think of the days that are before us. The days are present. Tomorrow is a different time.

Ruth's Promise

So, I truly am blessed. As I wrap up now and close my journal, I look upon my husband, who is tending to the grounds to grow food for us. I am in awe because I am a wife, one day, I shall be a mother.

Entry 6: It's been 10 Years

Where has the time gone?

It's been a long time since I have written in my journal.

I have been so busy being a wife, tending to the field, doing chores, laughing, and enjoying living in Moab. And being married.

It's been 10 years since I got married. Unfortunately, I am not with a child yet, but I still eagerly wait. But in those ten years, we have continued to live and be a family.

I would say that Naomi is no longer a foreigner to the Moabites or Moab. I can say my husband and my brother-in-law have adapted to the culture. But one thing has never changed. My mother-in-law's faith. She remains steadfast in God.
She has never gone to the right or the left. She has stayed in the presence of God, knowing that he is a faithful God.

Even as I write this right now, I must say I have learned and grown so much in the ways of my mother-in-law's teaching and the example that she showed in her relationship with God. Even my sister-in-law, Orpha, has learned from my mother-in-law's ways. She has become patient. This patience has taught us both to wait on our desires. Just like me, Orpha also has a desire to have children. We will wait, and little by little, it shall come to pass.

Entry 7: Being an Outcast

I have been so busy being married that I didn't have time to write in my journal.

Let me share a little bit more about my journey.

You know! being married, celebrating my husband, and celebrating the life we've led together has been so good. I would say there have been so many challenges living in Moab.

There were challenges.

My mother-in-law, Naomi, was an outcast and was treated as such quite often. But she had such grace and faith in God that at times she appeared unfazed. However, I think, at some point, it was wearing on her because, of course, we are still human, and being human, we still feel. We still feel the afflictions of men who are not pleased with you.

And again, the grace that my mother, Naomi, had was one for the eyes of those who could see the grace. I think it helped me mature and straighten my back more as a wife and a mother-to-be when I was treated differently for marrying an outsider.
Though I never met my father-in-law, I could see why he loved her.

I could see why her sons honored her.
It was more than just her culture, it was God's grace manifested through her.

Ruth's Promise

She was a nurturer, she was a role model, she was everything I adored. She was everything her sons would want in a wife.

I loved her.

I loved being married. I loved the time we spent together. And I'm very grateful that I can share this with you.

Whoever may read this, one day, I'm sure you too may be experiencing certain things. I think of some of my sisters and friends when they talk of their mothers-in-law and the relationship they desired to have with them, but never had. The ones that had those relationships sometimes had better relationships with their mothers-in-law than with their mothers.

Having balance isn't easy, but I am learning through Naomi's ways. But as I watch my mother-in-law, Naomi, she seems to have balance in her God, Yahweh. A balance that is unexplainable but quite visible. I hope to become this.

Many women, I, myself, have deep desires of the heart, and those desires sometimes take over and can be harmful to the outcome. The motives behind our desires are essential to our outcomes. Just because we want something doesn't mean we will have it. There are right and wrong motives behind our desires, and God will weed out what is not good for us. I am taking some time to examine my motives behind what I desire.

I'm happy I could share this entry.

I must go now because I have to fetch water from the well. And we will be baking bread for dinner. Mahlon will be home soon from working in the field. I can't wait to see him, the sweat on his brows from his labor, and the strength of his presence. His presence brings me such delight as he enters our home. I feel so secure when he is there, especially when he holds me in his arms.

Sometimes, I wonder if my sister, Orpah, feels the same way about my brother-in-law Chilion.

We live here together and embrace the time together. We laugh together. Orpah and I joke around. We do what girls do. But do we see love and the ways of life in the same way? I wonder? I must get ready to go. It is time for us to complete our chores.

We are about to fetch the water together, and we will have a nice conversation, both of us wishing and dreaming of the children we will have one day. I wonder who would be pregnant first. Whoever it is, we will celebrate the other. I will talk to you tomorrow.

Entry 8: My Husband, Mahlon

It's been a while. We have been married for quite some time, as I mentioned before.

Mahlon, my mother Naomi, and Chilion have been here in Moab for over ten years now. It's been a long time. The days have been good. There are moments when they grieve, and they miss their father. But daily, we pray, and we get through it. And God gives us the grace to get through it.

As I progress each day, I continue to learn how to be a wife to my husband and embrace the gift of marriage. It is a gift. Many may not think so, and some may think so, but I know it is a gift. It is not given to everyone. To those it is given, to it is a unique feeling, a sense of accomplishment, hope, togetherness, and peace that comes with marriage.

As we navigate throughout the days, I'm so excited because so much has happened. We've grown so much closer, and Mahlon is my best friend. And I love speaking to him. And I love being with him. But I am not pregnant yet, and I'm still waiting as we journey through these days.

It is such a gift that I have been given.

I will enter later on today. I have to go.

Entry 9: Test & Tribulation

As our days progressed, we had no idea what was before us. It just seemed like a peaceful day, doing our chores, laboring, enjoying the company of each other, and being a family. And the tenth year of my husband's move to Moab, everything would change.

It was the year that tragedy would fall upon our household yet again, but this time, I would be present for this fall.

Though I wasn't there the first time when their father died. I am here now. A dreadful illness has come over my husband and my brother-in-law. The weight of what is going on was frightening. My mother-in-law is fervently in prayer, seeking God for guidance and healing.

My sister-in-law, Orpah, and I are praying right beside her, believing that God could answer her and maybe us, even though we are Moabites. Nonetheless, we knelt with her and prayed. We took humble positions, praying for our husbands as they suffered through this illness and seeking healing from God.

We are women and strong among each other, but we have also experienced the reality that we live in a world without a husband, what shall we have and how shall we survive? Who will protect and provide?

What is this life for, Naomi, to experience such a thing again?
After the loss of her husband, she now has the frightening fear of possibly losing her sons.

Would I be like Naomi, a widow? Would I be alone? What would it be like for us to survive and manage?

There are so many questions that are going through my mind, and I will trust God with my whole heart. Yet I am fearful.

As each day progressed, Mahlon and Chilion grew sicker. We've sorted medicine and gone to the market a few times to, fetching herbs for tea, and rubbing medication but nothing has changed.

The worst has come to pass. They are struck with fever, unusual fragilities, weakness, and inability to get up and move.

What shall I do? I would do as my mother-in-law has always taught me. Pray and seek God.

Entry 10: The Uncertainty

I cry daily. Uncertainty and fear tried to choke the life out of me because I didn't know how to help my husband, my mother-in-law, or my brother-in-law, or even my sister-in-law.

I'm so fearful of what may come. My heart is so heavy, uncertain of what is next. The days are so different, and of course, in the village, in the marketplace where we go to fetch things, there are many rumors that Naomi's household has been struck again because they married outside of their custom. The saying was that our household was cursed because of marrying a Moabite, and a curse that has fallen upon them.

It is what they say. This is what they whisper, and sometimes they don't even whisper. They speak loud enough for us to hear. And then we walk back home with our heads down, saddened and unsure.

We are without children. What shall this become of us? How can I live without Mahlon? My heart is so heavy. My eyes are swollen from tears. I am unable to sleep, unable to eat, and even struggling with praying. I will remain on my knees like my mother-in-law.

Surely, the God of Naomi knows all things and can see all things.
Surely, the God of Naomi, Yahweh, has a plan. At this moment, we lean heavily on her and the way she believes in God.
We are learning. Her process is not easy. It's still quite new to us, but we are trusting.

There are so many tears every night. I try not to cry in front of the family. There was so much going on, so much uncertainty.

Ruth's Promise

I miss speaking to Mahlon the way we are used to. As he lay suffering, now the sweat on his brow is the sweat of illness rather than the sweat of labor and providing for his family.
He is unable to walk. I no longer see him walk through the doors with his brave arms and strength. His warm smile was washed away by pain. My strong tower lies fragile.

I must go, I hear something.

I hear mourning, I must go, I must go.

Entry 11: The Dreadful Cloud

It's been a sad time. Mahlon and Chilion have both passed away. There is a dreadful cloud over our household. Naomi is inconsolable. She has not moved. Her words are "God has dealt me a hard hand" and "God has dealt me a hard hand". Her pain, the joy of her smile, is no longer there.

I feel empty inside and broken. I did not know this would come to this. I have no strength. I am weak and am shaking, which I cannot control.

Orpah, she too, is inconsolable.

Our entire household—is it a curse? Is that what is coming over us? We are without husbands and children. We are with shame, fear, and uncertainty. I can't help but feel pity for us because we do not know what the plans are, and people are very cruel.

In Moabite. Moab, people are not as helpful and nurturing as Naomi.

Yahweh,

She can't even pray. I call upon you because you know best how to handle your daughter. We are not daughters of yours, but I seek a private prayer for all of us to give us strength.

My handshakes as I write this in disbelief that my husband is gone. My strength is gone. Pain has now become my company. Grief has taken over, and uncertainty is knocking at my door.

Ruth's Promise

What shall tomorrow look like?

When I dreamt of my marriage, I dreamt of having children.

What shall we do? What shall we do? And how shall we do it?

We have no means. We have some things stored away. But I do remember Naomi saying, "Jehova Jireh, our provider." Therefore, I believe he will provide for us. He will make his way out of nowhere. He will open a door that seems to be locked.

The strength that we need to keep going is not there right now.

I am stricken by my pain.

We are stricken by the emptiness of our home, that death has made its way to this household yet again.

Forgive us, Father, for whatever we have done against thee.

As I wake up from the long, painful night, the morning does not present comfort, though I do not want to be perceived as ungrateful. But the loss is heavy.

Naomi is up. I could hear her moving around, probably speaking to her father in the morning. Though we experience differences in losses, but similarities as well; how do you explain the loss of the children of her womb, and her husband?

Ruth's Promise

She was in a foreign land that she never wanted to come to in the first place. This is grieving as well.

I'm sure much regret befalls her.

Oh! Father, hear us as we wake up this morning from the night's pain, though the morning does not provide relief from the night. My mind is racing with the thought of my husband.

The thought of the life we created, the children we never had, the life that we never had to live.

I rested my eyes very late last night because I could hear Naomi's tears and my tears, and my sister-in-law's tears.

The house is filled with mourning and sadness.
Heaviness, loss. No husband, no covering, no protection.

Yahweh, why won't I turn my mind to you, knowing that you are the husband and the protector? You are the one who wraps your arms around us and gives us what we need for each day that comes.

The days are countless. The tears are many, the heaviness. We've lost our appetite. Our ability to rest, We labor, but labor for what? The Lord, send an answer. Send us away, tell us what we should do. You are the God of Naomi. You are the one she turned to when she lost her husband, and I saw joy in her when I met her. Not as if she didn't lose, but how much she trusted you.

Everything is dying around us. I had not realized that my husband's hands were the hands of five while ours were the hands of one.

Ruth's Promise

Lord, give us strength. Give us strength, Lord. I cry out to you because you are the only one who can hear us. Lord, hear our cry, hear our need for you.

Though the sun has risen, and it is warm on our faces. It feels so cold and lost and distant. I kneel before you, calling out to you, seeking you for your love and your mercy.

As I reflect on the days after my husband died, I often remember hearing my mother-in-law's tears in the background on her side of where we live, and as I listened, I cried even more.
I cried for my loss, but I also cried for hers.
I miss him so much. At times, I feel very weak and broken.
I feel a sense of emptiness because I do not have my partner and friend.

During these years, with losses in this household, we have felt a sense of pain that cannot be expressed in words. Even now, as I think about it, I am crying so many tears.

Even my sister's loss.

First, the loss of my husband, but also the loss of what our future looks like.

I don't know what is ahead of us. But I do know there is something in front of us. I don't know how we would come out of this, but I know God is the answer.

As we journeyed through this time, laying the bodies of our husbands to rest was even more dreadful and knocked us off our feet. Naomi wailing at the gravesite as their bodies are laid down was one I will never forget. The screams from the dept of Naomi's womb echoed in the air and touched every woman that was a mother and those who desired to be a mother. I wonder what life would be like if things were different.

I remember the days I was waiting for him to come home. And the sweat on his brows from laboring, excitement to see him, preparing a warm meal for him, creating the atmosphere for him to be at peace.
I remember those days when my sister-in-law, Mother Naomi and I would get together and pray for our household. Never did we think that we would be faced with death, darkness and grief that surpassed our understanding.

People are kind, and some are unkind.

People have come by to visit and have small conversations. Some people did not know what to say. Others called it a **curse**. People said it was because they married Moabites.

Their words were painful and hurtful.

I do not believe in my heart that God's love and the love he puts in us, bringing us together, would be cursed. But I am still foreign to their ways, but I believe His love is never a curse..

I have come to know some of the ways of Naomi's people through watching my mother-in-law. And as I journey through this process, I must trust God. I don't know Even as I say it, some may say that you trust the God that has taken your husband, father-in-law, and brother-in-law How could you trust a God that let this happen?

Yes, I see the God in Naomi despite her pain and mourning. I see the God that walked her through the loss of her husband and now THIS!

Ruth's Promise

Despite crying when she thinks we are asleep and we can hear her. She still bows before God's feet even still. Even if she questions, she still bows before his feet. She still knows God as the only answer. She still comes to God seeking answers.

She still comes to God, and who am I not to?
I will bow at His feet.

Entry 12: The Visitor

As we made our way to the marketplace with the little that we had left, Naomi overheard that there was a visitor to Moab from her hometown, Bethlehem. And he spoke of some things. He expressed that there was an overflow in Bethlehem, which once had a famine that led Naomi and her family to Moab.

She has decided to go back, and I cannot blame her.
She has never truly been welcomed in Moab. She was a Foreigner.

We are the Gentiles, and they are the Jews, the chosen people. But not chosen in the eyes of Moab, they don't exist and are not welcome.

Would God give us strength?

Bethlehem would be a new place for us, too.

We would go with our mother-in-law, who is now our mother. Although I think she has other plans for us. But I have decided to go with her, to serve the God that she serves.

These ten years, I have watched Naomi and how she has loved upon God and how God has loved upon her.

Many would say I was foolish because God dealt a hard hand, but the good hand that God has dealt far outweighs the hard hand. I will trust the God that she trusts. I will walk with her and follow her.

God gave her strength as we move on through our losses.

We still have to find the strength and the courage to keep pressing forward and to see life.

If there truly is plenty in Bethlehem, then that is where we would go to receive that which God has for us.

Entry 13: Returning To Bethlehem

Today was harsh. Today is the day I could hardly get up, I could barely eat, and mourning has taken over.
We are all scrunched over in pain from our loss.

Naomi came to speak to us today and explained that she is returning to Bethlehem after speaking to the gentleman from Bethlehem. And that Bethlehem is in the overflow, quite different when they came here empty.

She is willing to go home. She has seen that God has dealt with her hard. She is ready to go back amongst her people to what she knows, and I can't help but understand.

She said I do not feel confident in Moab. Bethlehem is what I know.

She also talked to us about going back to our mother's homes to find new husbands.

As you know, a husband is essential in our country. Having children is essential. Now, we have no husband and no children. Like wasted vessels.

Orpah and I have both decided to go with Mother Naomi. But she has refused. Orpah went back to be with her family.

I have decided to devote my life to Mother Naomi.

Ruth's Promise

I have decided to go with her, and that her God would be my God. And I have explained to her not to bid me to leave because I will not go. I will not go and leave her. It is what I know now. It is who I am.
I have learned so much from my mother-in-law in these short times. I could not leave her side. I am here to be with her. And I trust that it is all well for us.

God will make a way.

I see her as a mother. It is a difficult task to persuade her to understand that. To understand that we will not leave her.

She had even instructed us not to call her Naomi, to call her **MARA**. Ah! And the meaning behind that, the meaning behind it, is far greater than we could imagine.

Naomi's life was full of Joy. And now it is full of pain. She was able to come through after the loss of her husband, which took time, but now the pain is far too great. She has lost everything in her eyes.

Pain and grief are what we know now.

As I recount, her name means: Naomi's name means **HONEST BEAUTY**.
A pleasantness. And that is what I have always seen with her.

Now, with the mourning and deaths that we are experiencing. I am seeing another side to her. As I look, I see **MARA** means **BITTERNESS**.

Mother Naomi could no longer see the pleasant nature of herself.
She was bitter.

Ruth's Promise

After what had happened. Three losses: her children and her husband.

Now, her daughters-in-law are without children. Not even children to comfort but alone. The tears in her eyes, the redness, the fatigueness.

Some days, she does not get up. She lay in the place where she prayed and asked God to save her son's lives and God did not.

She feels as though her life is bitter. She stated that she went away full, but the Lord has brought her back empty.

She feels the Lord has afflicted her. And the almighty has brought misfortune unto her.
I allowed her to speak and just listen. But I let her know that I would not leave her.

I had to tell her, "Do not urge me to leave you or turn back from you". Where you go, I will go. Where you stay, I will stay. Your people will be my people, and your God my God. Where you die, I will die, and there I will be buried. May the Lord deal with me, be it ever so severely if even death separates me from you. And this is my heartfelt prayer, my words, my truth, my love for the God that she serves, and my love for her.

I believe deep in my soul that there is more to this than just what is in front of us: **bitterness**.
I take the posture of my mother-in-law when her husband died.

I have grief, I have pain, I mourn, I miss Mahlon. But I will not leave her. Some would say stay with your mother and have another husband. Others would say you are not from that town. You are not from Bethlehem. You can not go there. They will treat you cruelly.

Ruth's Promise

Not crueler than they have treated my mother-in-law here in Moab.

So, I lean not on my ways. I will trust the God that I began to know in my mother, Naomi's household. The God that carried her. The God that provided for her, the God that was with her. The God that gave her strength, the God that took care of us. The God that would take us through this journey to get back to Bethlehem.

Orpah decided not to go with us. I cannot choose for her or judge her. I was called for this journey with my mother Naomi.

Entry 14: Our Journey

We are on our journey. The roads are long. It is quite dangerous for women to be on the road alone.

Many things could happen. We could be enslaved, taken prisoner, or raped. Very dangerous, but I believe that God is watching over us. I know that he is.

I remember that my mother-in-law uses the term **El Shaddai,** which means all-sufficiency. I will trust God in the good and the bad.

Journeying to Bethlehem: Through this journey, the winds, the rocky roads, and not having enough provisions. We have each other. I have become the strength for my mother Naomi, and I am happy to be that for her.

I draw from the God that she serves. As we journey to our destination, I know I am fortunate to have him in our lives.

We made it through the dangers and rough roads. So, as we approach, we are entering Bethlehem during the **Barley Harvest**.

At the beginning of it, she taught me what it was. It is essential to understand that this is the time for new beginnings.

I don't know what that means. My mind is very set on finding work where I can get food for us to eat. We trust God even amid everything that is going on. Knowing that he has not forgotten us and he never will.

Barley Harvest.

Surely, I can find a field, you know, find a field where I could labor to find food for us. I am not sure where we are going to live. I know my mother Naomi has stated that there is land that belongs to her husband, which now belongs to my deceased husband. Now that he is gone, a woman cannot manage this on her own. So, we would need help.

I understand from my mother Naomi that the Barley season also represents **A SYMBOL OF A NEW LIFE AND RESURRECTION.** So I would believe God as such that we are entering Bethlehem at the time of the Barley season for a new life. I don't know what that new life looks
like. But we were entering it whether we were ready or not.

Entry 15: Laboring In a Field

As I write this, I am a little tired. I found a field of labor. I've been laboring in this field to bring some of the grain back that we may be able to eat.

Currently, we are staying in a cave-like shelter. We have done our best to prepare for it

As I recall, I went out early and let my mother, Naomi, know that I was going to the field to pick the leftover grains that were left behind by the harvesters.

I ended up in a field that I do not know. It was not too far off. Somehow, I was led there. As I labored in this field, there was grain for me to pick. It is quite dangerous to be in the fields as a woman and a foreigner, too. Dangers still tried to follow me, but I would trust God.

I worked as hard as I could. My hands felt brittle. They had calloused, but I worked. I did the best that I could. As I was there and far off, someone saw me.

And I keep trusting God.

Entry 16: The Kinsman Redeemer

As I share this, my hands shake, and my eyes are full of tears. The loss of my husband, I can feel his absence so strongly. I miss him.

Although we are vulnerable and uncovered, we must keep pressing on.

Mother Naomi feels the grief as a mother, but she also knows the grief as a widow and the grief for me as well. It reminds her of when she arrived in Moab as a foreigner, now I am the foreigner.
I miss my husband. I miss so many things.

I cry silently alone so I don't trigger my mother Naomi's grief, her mourning. But it comes quite often. Sometimes, I don't feel like I can breathe without him.

But time cannot be spent on my crying and mourning because we must find ways to earn a living, eat, and live in this new place in Bethlehem.

It allows me to know that this is where he grew up, this is where his life was, and this is the place that Naomi loved.

I am excited to be here. I am also sad. But I embrace the moments I can feel Mahlon's presence.

As I walk through this field where I labor, I find grain to feed and provide for us. A wonderful gentleman has helped us. I am excited to let Naomi know that I met him. As I describe him, she recognizes who he is. She has told me he is a relative of her husband's family.

Ruth's Promise

He is what they call a **KINSMAN REDEEMER**. With that being said, a kinsman redeemer is the one who will take on the responsibility of the father, brother, or son who has passed away. To take on his family or lineage to be responsible.

He seems so kind. He is so gentle in Spirit. I can see that he could truly be the kinsman redeemer.

I am grateful that I did end up in his field. It must be God

I am grateful that I can see what is in his field, the abundance in giving and receiving, and his kindness. He provided food for me to eat while I worked in the field. Strangely enough, as I labored, the grain that I would pick up behind the harvesters increased.

Entry 17: A Permanent Home

Mother Naomi explained to me that she felt it was time for me to have a permanent home. So, I might be provided for.

Ruth's Promise

In this life, women are unable to provide for themselves. I may say that I have been working in fields, and God has made provisions and given me the physical capacity to be able to provide somewhat for us. But we still need covering, continued provision, and shelter.

She explained that Boaz (the Kinsman redeemer), that's his name, a close relative, has been very kind by letting us gather grains with the young women. She explained that he would be at the winnowing Barley on the threshing floor.
She also stated that I needed to bathe, put on perfume, and put on a beautiful dress because his eyes had fallen upon me.

He had shown me a favor. Naomi saw him as the one who could become his wife. After all, he was the kinsman redeemer.

She suggested that I go to the threshing floor. But do not let Boaz see me until he has finished eating and drinking with other gentlemen there.

When night fell, it was unsafe for a woman to be there with the men on the threshing floor. Also, the rumors could spread. I was going to do as she told me.

I bathed, I put on perfume, and the nicest dress I could put together. Once I was there, she said that when he fell asleep, I would lie at his feet. And he would tell me what to do.
Naomi knew for certain that I had won favor in the sight of Boaz.

As I said to Naomi, I would do as she told me.

So I went to the threshing floor that night and followed the instructions my mother Naomi gave me.

Ruth's Promise

Boaz had finished eating and drinking. I could see it from afar off. He was in good Spirits. And then he went to lay down at the far end of the pile of grains and went to sleep. I quietly uncovered his feet and lay down as I was instructed to do.

Around midnight, Boaz suddenly woke up and turned over. He was surprised to find a woman lying at his feet. At first, he did not know it was me. Then, when his eyes were clear, he said, "It's you", and I answered. And I answered him, "Yes, my Lord, I am your servant, Ruth".
And I asked him to "spread the corner of your covering over me, for you are my family redeemer." He replied to me, "The Lord bless you, my daughter." You are showing even more family loyalty now than you did before, for you could have gone after a younger man, whether rich or poor."

Boaz was much older than I.

I didn't see his age. I saw his kindness.

Though he had age on his face, there was a gentleness in his face, it was his kindness that overshadowed everything. And I was grateful that he protected me.

He assured me not to worry about a thing. He said he would do whatever was necessary for everyone in town to know I was a virtuous woman.

While it was true that I was one of his family members, there was another relative, another man who was closer than he was.

He told me to stay the night at his feet, and in the morning, he would go and talk to him and see if he was willing to redeem me to him. He said that if the closer relative accepted the kinsman redeemer role, he would have to marry me, and there would be nothing Boaz could do.

He said he would redeem me for himself, but he told me to lie down until morning because it was dangerous for me to have been seen.

So, I lay down at his feet till the morning.
But I got up before the light was out, so no one would recognize me.

He said that no one should know that a woman was here on the threshing floor because it would spread so many rumors and so many things.

He told me to bring my cloth and spread it out. He measured six scoops of Barley into the cloth and placed it on my back. Then he returned to town.

He always made sure that I had more than enough.
I have never experienced such kindness.

Surely, Yahweh is making a way.

I remember my mother Naomi speaking of Yahweh being **Jehovah Jireh**. He is a provider.

He had provided Boaz. And all the provisions that came.

I didn't have to work as hard in the field because there were days when the sun was very heavy, but Boaz always gave me plenty for myself and my mother Naomi. His kindness extended far more than I would have imagined.

Ruth's Promise

However, he mentioned that I was even kinder and more loyal in what I had done; he was referring to my loyalty to my mother, Naomi. He, too, showed similar kindness to me.

I went back home to my mother, Naomi. She asked me in excitement what had happened. I told her everything that Boaz had done. I let her know that he gave me six scoops of Barley. He didn't want me to come back empty-handed to you. She said to be patient until we hear what happens.

Mother said;

The man will not rest until he has settled this matter today. Naomi was extremely knowledgeable. And I owe it all to her, and I am very grateful. I do not know what the outcome would be, but I will trust Yahweh, and I will trust his decision.

So, I'm thinking about everything my mother Naomi told me to do to prepare myself to go through the threshing floor.

I thought about a lot of things: I went and did what she told me, and it was successful, but I was fearful. I have never known another man or to lay at his feet other than Mahlon.

I have FEAR.

Well, I knew the character and kindness of Boaz in the field, but it did not mean that I didn't have fear. I was also a foreigner in Bethlehem.

If I were seen, it would ruin what was left of who I was. Many men may have looked at me and had an interest. Maybe they did not because I was a foreigner and feared I was a curse of being subject to death as the men in our family.

Ruth's Promise

I trusted Mother Naomi, I trusted her wisdom, I trusted her faith, I trusted everything that she was doing, and she told me her plans were good for me. There weren't too many ways to get ourselves out of the situation.

I wanted to be delivered, but was too tired to take that bath.
I was too tired to put on that perfume.
I was too tired to go to the threshing floor.

I wondered what Boaz thought when he woke up and saw me at his feet. Mother Naomi explained to me that It was their custom, and she said he would explain to me what to do next.
And I responded in the process. "I trusted what Boaz would do."

A man that I had one encounter with, but I had many provisions in the field because of him.

He always left something more for me. And somewhere in my heart, I knew Boaz was doing it for me. There were moments when I thought he was doing it for Naomi. Other times, I realized he was doing it for us both.

I believe Yahweh surely has something to do with this whole process.

I found favor in Boaz. The favor did not come because of the way I looked. I had a torn garment of clothing while in the field, my face was filthy and hunched over, but he still attended to me and provided for me. So surely it cannot be the outward appearance.

Boaz spoke of my character. He talked of my loyalty. He spoke of my ways that far outweighed my beauty.

Ah! Beauty would one day fade, but your character, heart, and service to Yahweh would never fade.

I reminisce about that day at the threshing floor. How I prepared myself. It was dark. I found a quiet area, behind a rock, to hide near the threshing floor. I kneeled and waited. I felt laughter. I could see the lands far off, men enjoying, drinking, and feeling merry. It was Barley. It was a time that was productive and flourishing. It was overflowing.

The gentlemen enjoyed themselves.

I must say, for a moment, I thought I was so different from all of the people in Bethlehem. I remember the times the women would get together at the well and talk about the day's affair, the marketplace, and the children.
I'm not very keen to do that in Bethlehem because I am a foreigner. But I remember doing that in Moab.

But as I sat and waited, I did not grow impatient. I was nervous, and I had a nut in my stomach. And then I prayed as my mother Naomi had. I prayed as God had shown up for me when I became a widow mourning the loss of my husband. He showed me a favor, and he has been kind.

He is the covering that women need.
It is the covering that Yahweh gives people that believe.
It is the covering of trust.

I had done as mother Naomi had told me. I trusted her faith. I trusted her wisdom. I put on my best garment and went to the threshing floor.

Ruth's Promise

As for me, I have never been around another man in that way except for my husband. But that day, I sat at the feet of my Kinsman redeemer, seeking his covering, his guidance.

Mother Naomi's God has become my God, and I know he will take care of me.

As I go and sit at the feet of Boaz, though I put on the garments, I know that it is not my outward appearance that captured his attention, and I gained favor in his sight. When he spoke to me, he talked of my loyalty and character. And because he did and knew me in this way, he provided for me and Naomi just as our Lord, who is our provider.

There are many men that I'm sure have noticed me. Many who wanted to speak to me may have even been afraid of my history. My husband dying, my father-in-law dying, my brother-in-law, almost as if we had a **curse** on us. Yet Boaz was not afraid of me and did not judge me.

I could not help but to think about Boaz. His face remained in my thoughts. There was kindness in his eyes. He had the character of a man who truly was honorable and honest. A man who served God. A man who lived a simple life.

I wonder sometimes if I could be the wife of another man. But I believe God has prepared a way for me, and the way began in the field. And now, we met at the threshing floor during the barley season at the feet of my future.

I shall trust God, who used Naomi to speak to me.
I shall trust the process.
I shall trust this journey that I am on.

Entry 18: The Meeting

This would be the day that morning when Boaz would meet with the closer relatives.

He went to the town at the gate where the leaders would sit. And they would reason and talk politics. The kinsman redeemer he had mentioned came over to sit down. He wanted to talk to him.

Ruth's Promise

Boaz called ten leaders from the town and asked them to sit as witnesses. In my time, there were witnesses for a transaction of this nature.

It wasn't just that it was my hand the person would have in marriage. They would also be responsible for the property that belonged to Mahlon, which originally belonged to my father-in-law.

As he had begun this process, women were not allowed there.
Mother Naomi and I watched from a distance. We could not hear anything but we could. Boaz let me know that he spoke to the closest kinsman. Boaz informed him that he would have to marry me. And he would have to also take the land.

He also let him know that should I be with a child, it would be recognized as Mahlon's child. The land would be for Mahlon's children.

This was the custom.

Boaz said to him, if you don't want it, let him know right away because he would be the next in line. He stated that the gentleman had said that he would do it until he realized there would be a cost because he would have to purchase the land from Naomi. The gentleman said he could not do it. It would endanger his estate because he would have to manage and pay for both.

In those days, it was a custom in Israel for anyone transferring a right of purchase to remove their sandals and hand them over to the other party. This publicly validates the transaction, and this is what they did before the ten leaders.
The other kinsman redeemer shrugged off his sandals, and he told Boaz to buy the land.

Ruth's Promise

Boaz was wealthy. He had the means and the ability to do so.

Boaz had no children. He was a man who had been by himself. He had never married.

Then Boaz made sure the elders, as far as we could see and the crowd standing around as we got closer, that they would witness today that he would purchase Naomi's property that belongs to her husband, and sons Mahlon, and Chilion, and the land he had acquired from Ruth, she was the widow of Mahlon, would be his wife. This way, she could have a son to carry on the family name of her dead husband and inherit the family's property here in his hometown. You are all witnesses. He stated.

It is amazing. Though Mahlon is not here, yet his legacy and his memories will remain.

The elders were all witnesses, and their response was, "May the Lord make this woman who is coming into your home like **Rachel** and **Leah**.

We all know Rachel and Leah married Jacob, who would later on become Israel. They built a nation of the 12 tribes of Israel, and they gave birth to many children, especially Leah. And from whom all the nation of Islam descended.

They also stated, "May you prosper and be famous in Bethlehem". May the Lord give you descendants by this young woman who would be like those of our ancestors, **Perez,** son of **Tamar** and **Judah**.

So, Boaz took Ruth home as his wife, and that was the day the ceremony happened.

We married immediately.

There was a ceremony very similar to the ceremony when I got married the first time. But there was something different about this.

Boaz was different. Boaz was my protector, my redeemer.

Boaz was willing to sacrifice everything to make sure that I would have everything I needed.

I became his wife when he slept with me, I became pregnant.

And there is so much more to tell. It is going to be a beautiful nine months. For the first time, I will carry a child in my loins.

Entry 19: Joy Restored

Ah! It's a new day here in Bethlehem.

I remember the days of my struggles.

I have found favor in your sight, Father. And you have displayed it through Boaz.
I have found comfort in my grief. And you have displayed it in the kindness of Boaz.

Ruth's Promise

I am full of your grace and I am humbled by the field that you provided for us.

Though my hand is not like the hand of a man who could be a side laborer, you gave me the back and the strength to labor nonetheless. And then you sent provisions, you cared for us, you wiped away our tears. You restored hope to my mother Naomi.

She no longer sees herself as **Mara. God turned our tears into joy**

What manner of man is this that he is so willing to be used by God to help us?

What I feel for Boaz differs from what I felt for Mahlon.
What I feel for Boaz, I feel it in the depth of my soul.

He is the kinsman redeemer.
He is the guardian, and he took on such a responsibility that most would shun and move away from. But his heart is full of love.

Oh! If I could share this with my sister-in-law and tell her what God has done.

Lord, Lord, I asked that I would be the wife to him, not just a heart's desire, but as a desire to fulfill his needs. And that I could return to him what he has given to us.
Lord, I ask you for your mercy, I ask you for your grace, I ask you for your strength.

You have removed the scales from my eyes, the heaviness from us, the ashes from us. Give me the strength, Lord.

I see the joy returning to my mother Naomi's eyes. That would only be you. I trust and know that all is well in your care.

The emptiness is fading away. The emptiness is fading away.

If I could share the excitement of my son leaping in my womb. Or maybe it's a daughter, there were such blessings behind this. Might I be able to have a child? There were so many blessings behind these moments. I embrace them with tears of joy in my eyes. I am excited.

This God, Yahweh, has taken my tears, pain, and hardship and turned it around for my good.

But if I could share the excitement of life in my womb.

I never thought I would have children because the dark days were there, but God has been faithful, and He made a way. He had a plan.

I throw my head back in delight, I feel the leaping of my child in my womb. As this child moves and grows, I prepare for a new life to be born.
Naomi and I bow down together daily, pray to our Lord, and express our gratitude to the Most High God.

It gives me strength to see her strength.

It encourages me to see her courage, to see her restoration, my restoration, and our deliverance.

As I watch her, as I've done for so many years, I am in awe of the woman she is, the woman that she has become. She has been my teacher, my mother, the one who ministers to me.

God is so gracious that God would bless beyond just what is in front of us.

If I could tell you the joy. And the delight on Naomi's face.

Women described and praised her. The words were, "Praise be to the Lord, who this day has not left you without a guardian-redeemer, may he become famous throughout Israel. He will renew your life and sustain you in your old age." "Your daughter-in-law, who loves you and who is better to you than seven sons, has given birth to him".

They described me as a daughter-in-law who was better to her than seven sons.

In their culture, as well as my own, having a son is highly esteemed. It is a compliment and an accomplishment. They saw me as an extraordinary woman. I, Ruth the Moabite, the widow, and once the woman without a child.

But I was the woman who loved my mother-in-law.

I was the woman who saw God in her even in her darkest moments.

I was the woman who would go where she went. Her God would be my God. Her ways would be my ways.

I was the woman that God assigned to be with Naomi.

I loved my mother-in-law.

Ruth's Promise

I remember my words to her, "Do not urge me to leave you or turn back from you. Where you go, I will go. Where you stay, I will stay. Your people would be my people, your God, my God.
Where you die, I will die, and there I will be buried. May the Lord deal with me, be it ever so seriously if even death separates you from me". My oath, my promise to Naomi, was from the depths of my heart. (Ruth 1:16-17) NIV.

I remember when she told them to call her **MARA** cause God has dealt harshly with her. But now, as I look at when she was born, Naomi's name, NAOMI, meant **JOY**. (Ruth 1:20) NIV.

Her joy has been reserved.
Her joy has been restored.

I wish I could tell this to many women, many young women, and any dying heart that may be faced with loss in different ways. God knows what he is doing, and he has not forgotten you.

I wish I could share this with them so that their hearts may be encouraged.

A girl from Moab, a Moabite, would marry a young man from Bethlehem. Not only would her husband die, her father-in-law, her brother-in-law, and three women were left desolate.

Different cultures came together. Everything seemed against us.

I wish I could tell a woman that leaving what she knows and going to a place that she does not know to serve a God named Yahweh would change her life for the better and that he would be faithful.

Ruth's Promise

I wish I could tell a woman when she is laboring with her hands and sometimes will see cuts and blisters on her hands, threading through fields that she knows nothing of, and experiencing uncertainty that God would be with her.

I wish I could tell a woman that, as she is working in a field, a man would show her kindness far more than any kindness she had experienced.

I wish I could tell a woman that a man would be a guardian-redeemer to her dead husband or something she lost in her life.

I wish I could tell a woman that despite the uncertainties of how much we would have to eat, where we would sleep, or the echoing tears from three different women of their losses and uncertainties, God would turn those tears into joy, that circumstance into redemption.

I wish I could tell a woman that she would be celebrated amongst other women and be called a woman who was greater than seven sons.

I wish I could tell a woman that her tears would be the water of a garden that would birth many things.

I wish I could tell a woman that she would be a bride yet again and be protected by her husband.

I wish I could tell a woman that the tears of my mother-in-law's eyes would be restored with joy.

I wish I could tell a woman that her womb, which echoed with emptiness, shall be filled with an **OBED, a promise**.

I wish I could tell a woman that there would be a legacy and lineage through my son.

I wish I could tell a woman that God has not forgotten you. God is the great Kinsman Redeemer.

I wish I could tell a woman to hold on just for a while longer, to stay at God's feet just a little while longer.

I wish. I pray that I could tell a woman, so her countenance could be lifted.
    I am Ruth, and this is my journey and journal.

The Scriptural Verses

Here are the Bible verses for each entry

The Entries	The Bible Verse
Entry 2: The Dream and Customs	Ruth chapter 1
Entry 3: Naomi's Way & Faith	Ruth chapter 1
Entry 4: Do It with Grace	Ruth chapter 1
Entry 5: Though I have a mother	Ruth chapter 1
Entry 6: It's been 10 Years	Ruth chapter 1
Entry 7: Being an Outcast	Ruth chapter 1
Entry 8: My Husband, Mahlon	Ruth chapter 1
Entry 9: Test & Tribulation	Ruth chapter 1
Entry 10: The Uncertainty	Ruth chapter 1
Entry 11: The Dreadful Cloud	Ruth chapter 1
Entry 12: The Visitor	Ruth chapter 1

Entry 13:	Returning to Bethlehem	Ruth chapter 1 & 2
Entry 14:	Our Journey	Ruth chapter 1 & 2
Entry 15:	Laboring In A Field	Ruth Chapter 2
Entry 16:	The Kinsman Redeemer,	Ruth chapter 2
Entry 17:	A Permanent Home	Ruth chapter 3
Entry 18:	The Meeting	Ruth chapter 4
Entry 19:	Joy Restored	Ruth chapter 4

Write your own Journal and leave a Legacy:

Ruth's story may resonate with many of you. Some of you may be entering a new chapter in your life or exiting a chapter that you thought would go one way, but you woke up one morning and it went another way. Some of you may have experienced so much sorrow and joy in the morning. This journal portion of the book is a great place to tell your story, unload the heaviness, and reflect on where you have been and where you are going. Your story can and will richly bless someone else, it is your testimony of how faithful God is. This journal is also a testament to you learning to trust God, Jesus, and the Holy Spirit. It is your walk. Let's get started with your journey and Journal. Let us begin:

Ruth's Promise

I will trust in the Lord at all times. "Trust in the Lord with all your heart and lean not on your understanding. Proverbs 3-5. (NIV).

My ways and God's ways, do they align?

Submit your plans to God. He will not fail you. Ruth is a testament to this. "In all your ways submit to him, and he will make your path straight." Proverbs 3:6. (NIV)

I am tired and restless. Can God help me?

God gives rest and comfort in our time of need. "Come to me, all you who are weary and burdened, and I will give you rest. Matthew 11:28. (NIV).

If I ask God, will He answer?

If you ask God and ask with the right intentions, and it aligns with the plans He has for you, you shall receive. "Ask and it will be given to you." Matthew 7:7. (NIV)

I have been seeking something specific in my life. Will God help me find it?

_____

God holds all things in His hands. "Seek and you will find." Matthew 7:8. (NIV).

I am afraid and filled with uncertainty.

God is with you through your fears and your uncertainties. "So do not fear, for I am with you; do not be dismayed, for I am your God." Isaiah 41:10 (NIV).

My tears are many.

God knows about your sorrows and He has purpose for them. "You keep track of all my sorrows. You have collected all my tears in a bottle. You have recorded each one in your book." Psalm 56:8. (NLT).

I am filled with Joy.

God will fill you with hope and Joy. Watch as God moves on your behalf. "May the God of Hope fill you with all joy and peace as you trust in him, so that you may overflow with hope by the power of the Holy Spirit." Romans 15:13 (NIV).

My rock, fortress, and deliverer

Did you know the Lord is a protector? he gives strength and safety. "The Lord is my rock and my fortress and my deliverer." Psalm 18:2 (KJV).

God, I need you to be my dependable force. Everything and everyone can fail, but not you.

God's words never return to Him void. If God said it, He will do it. "So shall my word be that goes out from my mouth; it shall not return to me empty, but it shall accomplish that which I purpose." Isaiah 55:11 (ESV).

You can tell God anything. Prayer is a conversation with God.

___

You can call on God at any time. Jesus met people where they were, and they spoke. "Call to me and I will answer you and tell you great and unsearchable things you do not know." Jeremiah 33:3 (NIV).

Today I woke up and felt….

It doesn't what you feel or see, all that matters is what you believe. "For we walk by faith, not by sight." 2 Corinthians 5:7 (NKJV).

God help me with my future:

God has a plan and a future for you that you do not have to figure out on your own. "For I know the plans I have for you," declares the Lord, plans to prosper you and not harm you, plans to give you hope and a future." Jeremiah 29:11 (NIV).

Lord, I desire a husband:

When you seek God first and align your heart with His plan, He will fulfill your desires. After all, He gives those desires. "Take delight in the Lord, and he will give you the desires of your heart." Psalm 37:4 (NIV).

Ruth's Promise

Lord, I struggle with doubt:

God will help you with your doubt. "Immediately, the boy's father exclaimed, 'I do believe; help me overcome my unbelief.'" Mark 9:24 (NIV).

Where Jesus meets you at your real

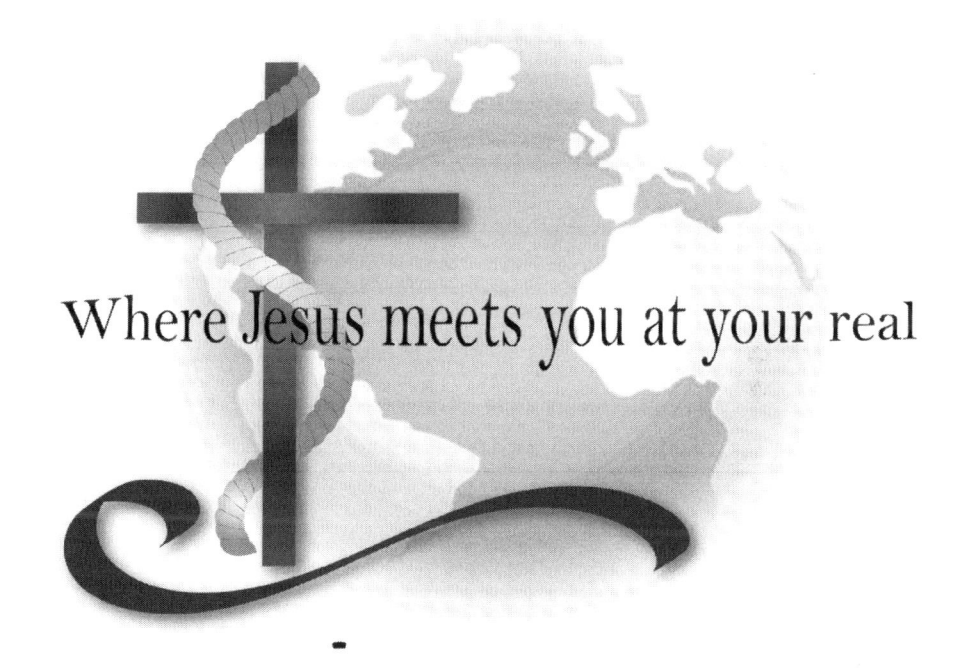

The Body of Christ, Youth & Adult Counseling Center, Corp

Ruth's Promise

Ruth's Promise

Bible Study Guide

Church Bible Study Tools:

Week 1 – The Journey Begins

Based on Ruth Chapter 1 & Entries 2–7 of Ruth's Promise

Theme: **Loyalty in the Midst of Loss**

Scripture Focus: Ruth 1:1-22

Opening Prayer

Lord, open our hearts as we study the beginning of Ruth's journey. Please help us understand the depth of loyalty, trust, and obedience even in uncertain times.

Summary of the Chapter

Ruth and Naomi suffer deep loss, yet Ruth chooses to leave her homeland to stay with Naomi. Her declaration, "Your people will be my people, and your God my God" (Ruth 1:16), marks the start of a faith-filled journey

Reflection Questions

• What emotions might Ruth have experienced leaving her home and family? What does she share in her journal?

- How do you relate to moments of transition or unfamiliarity in your own life?

- What does loyalty look like in your relationships?

Group Discussion Prompts

- How did Ruth's loyalty to Naomi reflect her character and values?

- In what ways have you seen God's faithfulness in your seasons of loss?

- What does it mean to trust God when the path ahead is uncertain?

Life Application

- Identify an area where God is asking you to walk by faith.

- Write a short prayer of surrender, like Ruth's, affirming your trust in God's path.

Memory Verse

"Your people will be my people and your God my God." – Ruth 1:16 (NIV)

Journaling Space

_____
_____
_____
_____
_____
_____
_____

Closing Prayer

God, thank You for Ruth's example. Give us the strength to follow You, even when the future is unclear. Help us love deeply and walk faithfully. Amen.

Leader Notes

• Encourage participants to read Ruth 1 aloud before the study.

• Allow space for emotional reflection—loss and transition are deeply personal.

• Invite testimonies or short journal readings inspired by Ruth's Promise.

God Bless

Pastor Natouchka L. Voigt
The Body of Christ Youth & Adult Counseling Center – Bcyacc1.org

Week 2 - Favor in the Fields The field may be a blessing.

Ruth Chapter 2

Theme: **God's Provision Through Unexpected Places**

Scripture Focus: "May the Lord repay you for what you have done. May you be richly rewarded by the

Lord..." - Ruth 2:12 (NIV)

Opening Prayer

Father, thank You for divine provision. Teach us to recognize Your hand even in ordinary places.

Summary of the Chapter

Ruth works in the fields to provide for Naomi. God leads her to Boaz's field, where she finds unexpected favor. This chapter shows how God meets needs faithfully.

Reflection Questions

- How do you see God's hand in daily provisions?
- What does favor mean to you in your current season?
- How does God use others to bless us?

Group Discussion Prompts

Ruth's Promise

- What stands out about Ruth's work ethic and humility?

- How has God placed you in a position of favor unexpectedly?

- In what ways has God provided for you recently?

Life Application

- Reflect on where God has placed you and look for His purpose there.

- Write a prayer thanking Him for daily provision and unexpected blessings.

Memory Verse

"May the Lord repay you for what you have done. May you be richly rewarded by the Lord..." - Ruth 2:12

(NIV)

Journaling Space:

_____
_____
_____
_____
_____
_____
_____
_____
_____
_____
_____
_____

Closing Prayer

Lord, thank You for showing us that You provide in all seasons. Help us to walk in gratitude and faith.

Leader Notes

- Have participants share recent testimonies of God's provision.

  - Encourage practical gratitude exercises like journaling blessings.

Pastor Natouchka L. Voigt

The Body of Christ Youth & Adult Counseling Center – Bcyacc1.org

Week 3 - Redeemed at the Threshing Floor

Ruth Chapter 3

Theme: Trusting God's Timing and Redemption

Scripture Focus: "All the people of my town know that you are a woman of noble character." - Ruth 3:11 (NIV)

Opening Prayer

Lord, we trust Your timing in all things. Teach us to wait in faith and obedience.

Summary of the Chapter

Naomi instructs Ruth to go to Boaz at the threshing floor. Ruth follows Naomi's counsel, and Boaz honors her request with integrity. This chapter reflects submission, trust, and honor.

Reflection Questions

- How do you respond when asked to wait or act by faith?
- What does submission to godly counsel look like in your life?
- Where is God calling you to trust Him more deeply?

Ruth's Promise

Group Discussion Prompts

- How does Ruth's approach show wisdom and honor?

- What does this chapter teach us about trusting the process?

- How do you handle seasons where the outcome isn't guaranteed?

Life Application

- Surrender a current concern to God and commit to wait on His direction.

- Write a letter to God expressing your trust in His timing.

Memory Verse

"All the people of my town know that you are a woman of noble character." - Ruth 3:11 (NIV)

Journaling Space

_____
_____
_____
_____
_____
_____
_____
_____
_____
_____
_____
_____
_____

Ruth's Promise

Closing Prayer

God, give us grace to walk uprightly and wait on Your promises. Let us be found faithful and full of hope.

Leader Notes

Invite group members to share how they've trusted God through waiting seasons.

Discuss examples of integrity and submission in biblical stories.

Pastor Natouchka L. Voigt

The Body of Christ Youth & Adult Counseling Center – Bcyacc1.org

Week 4 - The Fulfillment of Promise

Ruth Chapter 4

Theme: **From Brokenness to Blessing**

Scripture Focus: "Praise be to the Lord, who this day has not left you without a guardian-redeemer." - Ruth 4:14 (NIV)

Opening Prayer

Lord, thank You for fulfilling Your promises and redeeming every broken place.

Summary of the Chapter

Boaz redeems Ruth, they marry, and Ruth becomes the great-grandmother of King David. God turns mourning into legacy, showing that He restores and honors faithfulness.

Reflection Questions

- Where have you seen God bring restoration in your life? Where do you hope to see restoration?

- What legacy do you want to leave behind?

- How do you see God using your past for His glory?

Group Discussion Prompts

- How does Ruth's story encourage you in your current journey?
- What does it mean to be part of God's redemptive plan?
- How can we support others walking through loss into promise?

Life Application

- Celebrate a fulfilled promise or a healing God has done in your life.
- Journal a vision of the legacy you believe God is shaping in you.

Memory Verse

"Praise be to the Lord, who this day has not left you without a guardian-redeemer." - Ruth 4:14 (NIV)

Journaling Space:

_____
_____
_____
_____
_____
_____
_____
_____
_____
_____
_____
_____
_____

Closing Prayer

Thank You, God, for redemption. You turn sorrow into joy and pain into purpose. We trust Your hand in all things.

Leader Notes

Celebrate with the group how far they've come through the study.

Encourage personal testimonies and prayers of legacy and purpose

Pastor Natouchka L. Voigt

The Body of Christ Youth & Adult Counseling Center – Bcyacc1.org

A Heartfelt Thank You

Dear Reader,

Thank you for purchasing **Ruth's Promise: A Tale of Loyalty, Love, and God's Faithfulness.** I pray that Ruth's journey has blessed, strengthened, and inspired you to trust God more deeply in every chapter of your own life. Her story is not just one of history- it is a living testimony of divine providence, redemption, and unshakable loyalty.

I also invite you to learn more about the ministry behind this work. The Body of Christ, Youth & Adult Counseling Center, Corp. (BCYACC) has been serving communities with compassion and purpose since 2005. What began as a local outreach has grown into a global ministry, touching the lives of young families, the elderly, women, men, and those in need of hope and healing.

As the founder and a pastor, it is my honor to lead this Christ-centered work-helping individuals from all walks of life know the love of God, walk in freedom, and fulfill their purpose. Whether through counseling, wellness care, housing support, or spiritual development, our mission is rooted in love and built on service.

May the Lord richly bless you, and may Ruth's story continue to echo in your heart as a promise of God's unchanging faithfulness.

With gratitude,

Pastor Natouchka Voigt

Pastor Natouchka L. Voigt

Founder & Minister, BCYACC

The Body of Christ, Youth & Adult Counseling Center, Corp. | www.bcyacc1.org

TO LEARN MORE, PARTNER WITH US, OR GET INVOLVED, PLEASE VISIT: **WWW.BCYACC1.ORG**

Made in the USA
Columbia, SC
18 June 2025

6a3716d0-0524-4b8f-980f-3b6fe5119770R01